How to prepare for the tests

Remember!

- Everyone else is worried, too.

- Read the whole paper through.

- Spend some time on planning what you write before you actually start writing. It makes it much more likely that your work will make sense!

- Keep to the times that are allocated for each question. Don't spend too long on one question just because you can answer it, and then leave yourself with no time to answer a harder question.

- Remember that some questions are only tests of reading. That means that there are no marks for spelling, punctuation or grammar. Don't spend too long making your answers to these questions look neat and tidy. Concentrate on showing the examiner that you understand the passage and the question. But some questions are tests of writing. There are lots of marks available for spelling, punctuation, grammar and clarity of expression for these questions. You will need to check what you write for these answers.

- There will be some things you don't understand. Some of them will get clearer as you work on, but there might be some things that you will never understand. Don't panic. Make sure you tell the examiners what you **do** know: they are trained to reward you for what you can do, not punish you for what you can't.

Good luck!

What you need to know

Over the next few pages you can see examples of three different kinds of question that you might be asked about fiction.

1 You might be asked questions about a particular **character**:
   - What impression did you get of Mark's attitude towards school?
   - What do we learn about Emily in this extract?
   - How does the caretaker feel about the children at the school?

2 You might be asked questions about the **relationship** between characters:
   - What does the reader learn about the relationship between Mr Turner and his son?

3 You might be asked questions about the writer's **style**:
   - How does the author describe the changes in Alfred's feelings as the story develops?
   - What impression do you get of the school from the way the author describes it?

Examiner's tips

tip 1 Use a pencil in the exam to underline important words and phrases in the story.

tip 2 If it is a character's name that is mentioned, underline the main points in the story which are about that character.

tip 3 If the words 'attitude' or 'feelings' are used, underline the words that suggest the character's emotions.

tip 4 If it is a relationship between two people that is mentioned, underline everything that shows how they feel about each other.

tip 5 If the question is about the author's way of writing, or style, underline words and phrases that stand out and suggest to you that the author has really thought about them before writing. Now read this passage carefully.

NATIONAL TESTS

Paul Evans
Jane Lodge

Contents

This book will help you to revise all the skills you will need in the Key Stage 3 National Tests (SATs) for English. You will take the English tests at the beginning of May in Year 9.

Your papers will be taken away to be marked. Each question will be given its own mark. All the marks will be added together and you will be given a National Curriculum level for the tests as a whole. Your papers will be returned to your school, so that the marks can be checked.

Your teacher will also give you a National Curriculum level, based on your performance in English at school. The level from the tests and the level from your teacher will be put together to make the level that you will be awarded for English on leaving Key Stage 3.

How to use this book

This book will help you to revise all the skills you will need to do well in the tests. If you work through the book in the order we have set out, you will also get an idea of what the tests will actually be like.

Occasionally, we have mentioned National Curriculum levels, and the kind of answers you will need to give to gain certain levels. Don't concentrate on the levels too much. It is much more important that you try to raise the standard of your skills. In other words, say to yourself: 'This is the kind of answer I would give here and now – What do I have to do to improve my answer?'

Remember that there are people around you who want to help you make the most of these tests; don't forget to ask for their help and advice.

Character

Rosie's three brothers had all grown up and gone to sea. Her two sisters had married. Rosie was the last of the clan. She had entered the world when her father had been close to sixty and her mother in her early fifties. For all that, she was hardly the studious or scholarly type.

Rosie had little use for girls, and as far as possible avoided them. She had less use for boys, but found it undesirable to avoid them. That is to say, she made it a point to take part in everything the boys did. She was always on hand, and always the first to take up any daring or crazy idea. Everybody felt awkward about her continuous presence but it was no use trying to chase her away, because that meant a fight in which she asked no quarter, and gave none.

From *The Great Leapfrog Contest*, by William Saroyan

Example

What impression do you get of Rosie?
In your answer you should comment on:
- the way she behaves with boys;
- any facts that you learn about her personality.

Examiner's tips

tip 1   Underline the words and phrases that will help you to answer the question.

tip 2   Now write out your answer. Do not write too much but do cover all the points that you have picked up in your underlining. You will only have about ten minutes to spend on this question.

tip 3   Before moving on, read through your answer to check that it makes sense. Quickly make any alterations necessary.

tip 4   There are no marks given in this question for spelling and punctuation, but your writing should be clear.

Relationships

Read this passage carefully

…Joe Mortimer would divide the money exactly in half. Solemnly, from the very beginning of their marriage, he would put one half into a tin cash box and then push the other across to his wife, who took it from him with long, uneager hands.

'You know what that's for,' he would say, 'put it away.'

At first they were quite sure about children … Mrs Mortimer thought of children laughing and running among flocks of hens, scattering grain, tossing it among the snapping, quarrelling brown feathers …That was the sort of thing children always loved, she thought…

Then gradually, as time went by and there were no children, he became resigned to it in a puzzled, absent kind of way. It did not embitter him. If there were no children there were no children, he thought. …

But his wife could not see it like that. It was not simply that she wanted children; it was not merely a question of pride. It was a woman's duty to have children; it was all of a woman's life to give birth. It was a failure in her living. It was like a hen that did not lay eggs or a cow that was sterile or a tree that never came into blossom. There was no point in the existence of them.

As time went on she drew more and more into herself.

From *The Good Corn* by H.E.Bates

Example

What impression do you get about the relationship between Mr and Mrs Mortimer?

In your answer you should comment on:
* how they feel at the beginning of their relationship about each other and about children;
* how and why their feelings change.

Examiner's tips

tip 1 Use what you have learned about your own level of achievement to realise at what level you now answer questions. Try and reach the next level by following the advice given below. For example,
If you know that you now answer questions at level five, try to answer the question on this page at level six.

tip 2 An answer at level 5 will not only pick out the right parts of the passage but will also comment on the parts that have been selected. For example,
It says in the passage that at first they were quite sure about children. This tells me that they both thought it would be easy to have children.

tip 3 An answer at level 6 will comment on words and phrases from the text in more detail. It will also sound like the work of someone who has a clear opinion of their own. For example,
I think that the woman is more sad than her husband because he 'became resigned to it' and she 'drew more and more into herself'.

tip 4 An answer at level 7 will cover ALL points in detail and will talk about what the author is really suggesting. For example,
The author uses the words 'uneager hands' in the first paragraph and this suggests that they are not happy together. The lack of children seems to drive them further apart, as suggested by the last sentence.

Style

The question you have to answer might look like this (you will need to re-read the passage on page 5).

How does the writer make you increasingly aware of Rosie's personality?
In your answer you should comment on:
- the way her family situation is explained;
- the way her relationships with other children are described.

Or it might look like this (you will need to re-read the passage on page 6).

How does the writer make you increasingly aware of Mr and Mrs Mortimer's problems?
In your answer you should comment on:
- how they are described when they look forward to children
- how they are described when they know they cannot have children
- how the author traces the change.

Examiner's tips

To do as well as possible, you will need to:
- keep to facts that are relevant to the question;
- explain what you say;
- explain the main points, showing that you understand the passage;
- quote from the passage;
- write about words and phrases the author uses and the effects those words create;
- comment in detail on some points;
- write about words and phrases and why the the author uses them;
- show personal opinion;
- answer the question in full;
- give a personal opinion and say why you have that opinion;
- use quotations to show that you understand the effects of the writer's use of language.

Tortoise   by David Speechley

Lumbering carefully over stone and earth,
  Edging, stumbling, groping blindly,
To the favourite place of Michaelmas daisies.
  His food finished, now the tortoise
Feels his way one foot after another,
  Choosing a path among the grass,
Which looks like willows hovering high above his hard shell.
  Afternoon appears, sleep overpowers the beast.
Making heavy footsteps the tortoise finds a sleeping-place,
  One eye closes and the scum of the eyelid passes over both eyes,
The tortoise falls into a shelled sleep.
  Dawn; and he trundles off to find food,
He claws his way over the rockery,
  Which appears to him to be like the Andes,
Passing through glades of raspberries;
  And at last he finds his food,
Lettuce!
Clumsily he opens his leather-hard jaws,
  Draws his fire-red tongue out,
Then, with a churning of cranking and creaking efforts,
  He closes his mouth upon the lettuce;
Tortoise now returns and digs with great speed,
  To hide himself from winter.
The hole dug, he retreats in his creaking wet-covered shell,
  To sleep.

Example

How does the poem suggest the problems and pleasures of the tortoise's life?
In your writing you should comment on:
- what the poem suggests about the difficulties of the tortoise's life;
- what the poem suggests about the pleasures of the tortoise's life;
- how the poet uses language to bring the situation to life;
- your ideas on why the poet wanted to write this poem.

Now make some notes about the poem 'Tortoise' on page 9 before you look at the sample notes below.

About

This poem is about a tortoise and how he moves and what he eats. He goes to sleep for the winter at the end of the poem.

Poet's Message

The poet seems to like the tortoise and wants the reader to understand more about what it is like. He seems to have looked at the animal very carefully.

Refer to text

The poem says, '...the scum of the eyelid passes over both eyes'. This makes me think that the poet must have been watching the tortoise very closely. The words 'He claws his way over the rockery' help the reader to picture the way the tortoise moves.

I Like

I like the line 'Draws his fire-red tongue out' because I have seen a tortoise open its mouth and the tongue is funny. I like the words 'cranking and creaking' because they help me to see how hard it is for the animal to move.

Language

The use of the simile 'like willows hovering high above his hard shell' is effective because it emphasises how small the animal is. The grass bows over him like willow trees would over us. Many interesting verbs are used, e.g. 'stumbling', 'groping', 'trundles' and 'retreats' and they all help to describe the way the animal moves and eats.

Now find another poem and use the mnemonic to make notes about what that poem means.

Answer

The following answer to the question on page 9 is reasonably full and focuses on the bullet points given in the question. It also develops some points in detail and shows a clear understanding of how the language used by the poet makes an impression on the reader. The answer also gives the examiner a personal opinion about the poem and refers well to the text.

From the first word of the poem, 'Lumbering', the reader understands that the tortoise finds moving around difficult. All the verbs from then on show us more about the difficulties that the animal faces. He is described as 'stumbling' as though he cannot walk, and the verb 'groping' suggests that he cannot see. This idea is developed by the words 'Feels his way' in line 5. It must be very difficult for the tortoise to find food when he has difficulty walking and cannot see.

The rockery is described as being like 'the Andes' to the tortoise, suggesting how hard it is for him to move over it. Closing his mouth on the lettuce is described as an 'effort' which again makes me see how hard it must be for him.

The pleasures of the tortoise's life are sleeping and being near the Michaelmas daisies. He obviously enjoys his lettuce from the effort he puts into getting it. I know that sleep is important to him because of the number of times that it is referred to. The last line says 'To sleep' suggesting that sleeping is the best thing at this point in the tortoise's life.

I like the simile used to describe the way the grass bends over the animal's back, 'like willows hovering', because it sounds gentle and pretty. The poet seems to like tortoises and writes about this one in so much detail that I think he was watching one in his own garden. The poet is trying to make readers like the tortoise by making us sympathise with the difficulties that it has and by showing us each detail of the animal. I think he succeeds in this. The language he uses works well, particularly the verbs because they show the effort that the tortoise puts into living and the pleasure that it gets out of sleeping and eating.

If the question you have to answer is about an advertisement, it will look something like this.

Read the advertisement you have been given.

It is trying to persuade people to take a cruise in the Indian Ocean.

Scattered across the Indian Ocean lie islands with the finest white sand and the clearest crystal blue waters. These are the Maldives. Over 1000 coral islands, just 50 with hotels. Leave the main islands behind and cruise to the lesser known atolls, aboard the 74-cabin ISLAND EXPLORER.

THE 'UNDISCOVERED' ISLANDS of the MALDIVES

A 7 night Indian Ocean cruise from £699 including all meals

Day 1 Sunday
Non-stop DC10 flight from Gatwick to Male.
Day 2 Monday Male/Laguna
Afternoon arrival. Transfer to the ISLAND EXPLORER, lying off Laguna Beach.
Day 3 Tuesday Raa Atoll
The 'adventure' begins, as you cruise to the fascinating Raa Atoll. As you sail early for the island of Ifuru look out for the dolphins which often swim along with the ship. This is a large, uninhabited island with white sandy beaches, lush vegetation, a beautiful calm lagoon and excellent snorkelling. Barbecue dinner on Ifuru.
Day 4 Wednesday Ifuru/Ungoofaaru
Cruise to Ungoofaaru, the main inhabited island of the Raa group. In the afternoon, visit the island, seeing the village life including the building of local boats (dhonis).
Day 5 Thursday Ungoofaaru/Kudakurathu
Sail to Kudakurathu and spend a full day on this desert island. Enjoy a picnic lunch and relax on the beaches. You may choose to hire a local sailing boat or windsurfer.
Day 6 Friday Kudakurathu/Baa Atoll
Cruise to Kamadoo, in the Baa Atoll. Here you will find the life of a typical small Maldivian fishing village.
Day 7 Saturday Kamadoo/Male
Cruise to Kurumba with time this afternoon to visit the capital, Male, for shopping. The Captain's Dinner takes place tonight.
Day 8 Sunday Kurumba
Today enjoy the opportunity to relax at the resort island of Kurumba.
Day 9 Monday Male/Gatwick
Early afternoon flight to Gatwick, arriving later the same day OR you may choose to extend your stay at Blue Lagoon on Kuramathi or at Full Moon Beach.

BLUE LAGOON
An excellent medium class hotel with just 50 rooms, in a quiet location at one end of the island of Kuramathi. Restaurant, bar, coffee shop. Tennis courts, watersports, diving. Simply furnished rooms with airconditioning, ceiling fan, minibar, shower/wc. 2 hours by fast boat from the airport. Seaplane transfers: £49 supplement each way.

THE ISLAND EXPLORER
Built, and previously operated, in Norway, the delightful, medium class, ISLAND EXPLORER was completely renovated in November 1996 before commencing her Maldives programme. The number of cabins has been reduced to just 74 and full airconditioning has been added.

She is the first cruise ship of her kind to be dedicated entirely to cruising within the islands and the itinerary is designed to allow visitors a glimpse into the life of 'real' Maldives: where boatbuilding and fishing, rather than tourism, are the mainstay of the area; where traditional, little-known crafts such as lacquer work are being revived. And to totally uninhabited 'desert' islands. The islands here are a revelation for their natural beauty and interest, and are rarely seen by overseas visitors.

FACTS:

Length: 260 feet	**Swimming pool:** 1
Tonnage: 2611	**No of decks:** 5
Restaurant: 1	**Coffee shop:** 1
Bars: 2	**Lounge:** 1 main/1 smaller

Cabins (all non-smoking) are simply and attractively furnished and have 2 lower beds, private shower/wc (all supplements shown below are for the full 7 nights).

Inside deluxe: A or B deck (included in the price)
Outside deluxe: B deck: supplement from £84
Outside deluxe: A deck: supplement from £119
Outside deluxe: Saloon deck: supplement from £189
Outside deluxe: Boat deck: from £245
Suite: Boat deck. One double bed, sitting area. Supplement from £378 (NB: only 2 suites of this type).

FULL MOON
Full Moon is a 1st class resort with excellent facilities: choice of restaurants, coffee shop, freshwater swimming pool with an impressive sundeck overlooking the sea, tennis courts, watersports/dive centre. Rooms are in 2-storey, 4-room units, close to the beach, with airconditioning, tea/coffee making, minibar, phone, bath/shower. Water bungalows, on stilts over the sea, are available at a supplement. Transfer: 30 minutes by fast boat.

ALTERNATIVE FLIGHTS:
Fly on award winning Emirates (via Dubai). Supplement from £25 – £135.

Departure date:		Price:
28 Sep, 12 Oct '98	*Monday departure*	£969
26 Oct	*6 night departure*	£699
01,08 Nov		£799
22 Nov		£749
29 Nov, 06 Dec		£699
03,10 Jan '99		£899
14 Feb		£979
21 Mar		£899
04 Apr		£1049
02,09 May		£799
06,13 Jun		£699

NO SUPPLEMENT FOR THE SOLO TRAVELLER:
7 night cruise: May/June '99.
Inside deluxe cabins only (limited availability).
NB: we regret that children under the age of 12 are not accepted on this cruise.

14 night cruise/stay from £899
A 7 night cruise plus 7 night island stay is available:
Blue Lagoon (inc full breakfast/dinner): from £1049
Full Moon (inc full breakfast): from £899

The price includes: Return flights Gatwick/Maldives. UK Govt dept tax of £20. 7 night cruise including all meals and visits/excursions as described. Transfers. Prices per person sharing twin cabin. **Not included:** Local dept tax: approx $10. Optional insurance: £33 (7 nts); £55 (14 nts). Booking conditions apply.

To book, telephone (open daily inc Sat/Sun):

The Travel Collection
A trading division of Kuoni Travel Ltd

01306 744300

Deepdene House, Dorking, Surrey RH5 4AZ
Fax: 01306 744334 ATOL 132 ABTA V258X

How does the advertisement try to persuade people to go on the cruise?

In your answer you should comment on:

- how the writer describes the cruise and the places it will visit;
- the way words and layout are used to try to create a positive image of the cruise;
- whether you think the advertisement will succeed in persuading people to go on the cruise.

Examiner's tips

tip 1   Start by underlining 'persuasive' words in the text – words like 'finest white sand' and 'crystal blue waters'. Now write about these words and phrases and the effect that the writer wants to have on the reader. For example, you could write something like this.

By using the phrases, 'finest white sand' and 'crystal blue waters', the writer is trying to create the impression that this cruise will visit Paradise, a place where there is no pollution and no over-crowding.

tip 2   Now write about the effect that the photographs have.

The main photograph stands out from the text. It draws the eye of the reader and it leaves an impression of calm and sunshine and cleanliness which lasts in the reader's mind all the time he or she is reading the advertisement. The smaller photograph shows the cruiser and makes it look large and reliable and luxurious.

tip 3   Now write about the layout of the advertisement.

Photographs take up about a third of the space. The headlines are against a dark background, which makes them stand out. The main headline emphasises what the main photograph shows: that the islands are 'undiscovered', so that if you go there you will be able to enjoy peace and quiet. The second headline tells you the price, so that you do not have to search through the whole advert to find this out. It gives an impression of honesty and the idea that the company is proud that their prices are so low. All the information in the advert is divided into blocks, so that you do not have to read too much at once.

tip 4   Now write about whether you think the advert will persuade people to go on the cruise. You might write about what it leaves out, for example the people who live there. Again, quote words and phrases and say why you think they are or are not effective in persuading people to go on the cruise.

Now write your answer to the question. Refer to words and phrases in the advertisement to support your ideas.

You need to be able to write about how grammar has been used to create particular effects both in fiction writing and in non-fiction writing. To do this you need to revise the names of different functions of words within sentences.

What you need to know

1 **Nouns** are the names of objects, people or places.
Names of objects are called **common nouns**, e.g. *table, chair.*
Names of people and places are called **proper nouns**, e.g. *London, Wayne.*
Words naming abstract ideas like *justice* and *anger* are called **abstract nouns**.
Words naming groups are called **collective nouns**.

2 **Pronouns** can be used in the place of nouns, e.g. *Peter is a pony.* He *is good.*
Sally was cross. She *knew* she *had done wrong.*
The problem grew worse. It *was awful.* It *scared her.*

3 **Adjectives** tell you more about nouns, e.g. *The* old, wooden *house.*
The adjectives 'old' and 'wooden' tell you what kind of house it is.

4 **Verbs** tell you what kind of action took place and a verb changes form to show present, past, and future tense, e.g.
I run *home* – present
I ran *home* – past
I will run *home* – future.
Verbs must also agree with the **subject** of a sentence. The subject tells you who is doing the action, e.g. *Sally* eats *the cake.*
Here Sally, the subject, is singular, so the verb ends in an 's'.
They eat *the cake.*
Here, 'They', the subject, is plural, so the verb does not end in an 's'.

5 **Adverbs** tell you more about the action. They describe verbs. They tell you where, when, how and to what degree something was done, e.g.
He hit the ball hard.
He hit the ball home.
He hit the ball swiftly.
He hit the ball very hard.

Quick Questions

1 Write down three common nouns.

2 Give two examples of proper nouns.

3 Give two examples of abstract nouns.

4 Give two examples of collective nouns.

5 Write a sentence that starts with a proper noun and then a sentence about the same noun but which begins with a pronoun.

6 Can you think of a reason why pronouns are used?

7 Write a sentence that contains three adjectives. Notice that you must use a comma when you write more than one adjective in a list.

8 Copy out and fill in the following gaps:
   Verbs tell us what .... took place and change to agree with the..................... that did the action. The form of the verb also shows .... an action took place, e.g. past, present or future.
   Adverbs tell us more about the ....

9 Copy out and underline the adverbs in the following passage:
   The boy ran home. He ran quickly because he was scared. His heart thumped very loudly. He told me about it yesterday.

Now you can apply your revision to the text.
Go back to page 5 and read the passage again.

What do you notice about the use of proper nouns and pronouns to achieve the purpose?

Answer

The proper noun 'Rosie' is used at the start of sentences. This tells the reader that they are to focus on her. This idea is backed up by the use of the pronoun 'she' at the start of many other sentences. The passage is all about Rosie and the writer makes this clear by using words in this way.

Now try these questions about the passage on page 6.

1   What is the importance of the adverb in the first paragraph?
2   What do you notice about the way verbs are used in the third paragraph?
3   Identify two adjectives used to describe Joe Mortimer's reaction to the lack of children and say what they add to your understanding of the character.
4   Identify the repeated use of a pronoun in the last but one paragraph and say how it helps to achieve the writer's purpose.

You will find answers to these questions below. Do not read them until you have finished your own attempts.

Answers

Remember that your answers may be different, but you must show you understand the writer's choice of language and the effect of the language on the reader.

1   The adverb 'Solemnly', is used at the start of a sentence. This suggests it is important as adverbs often appear at the end of sentences. It tells us how Joe Mortimer gave the money to his wife. If the writer had used a different adverb, for instance, 'merrily', the meaning would have been completely changed. 'Solemnly' sets the scene for how important having children was to the couple.

2   There are many verbs in the third paragraph, e.g. laughing, running, scattering, and they all tell us what the children would be doing if they were there. By using so many verbs we can almost see the children filling the quiet lives of the couple and this stresses the fact that there are no children to perform these actions.They could be doing all this but in fact nothing is happening. It makes the reader sad.

3   The two adjectives used to descibe Joe's reaction are 'puzzled' and 'absent'. They both sound vague, as if he is not terribly upset. They tell us that he did not understand why there were no children and the adjective 'absent' suggests he somehow removed himself from the problem and got on with his life.

4   The pronoun 'it' is repeated in the last but one paragraph. It is used at the start of many of the sentences. This helps to show the importance of the lack of children to Mrs Mortimer. The 'it' refers to her inability to have children and the repetition of the word shows how this failure became more and more important to her.

You may be asked to comment on non-fiction texts rather than fiction. You should practise doing this with instructions, reports and advertisements.

In those sections of the papers identified as writing and in the Shakespeare section, your work will be marked twice: once for the content of what you say and once for technical accuracy in spelling, punctuation and grammar.

What you need to know

1 'i' before 'e' except after 'c'.

2 Dropping the final 'e'. Words ending in a silent 'e' drop the 'e' before adding a suffix beginning with a vowel, e.g. hope, hoping, hoped.

3 Keep the final 'e' if you need to keep the *s* or *j* sounds on words ending in 'ce' or 'ge'. For example,
service, serviceable;
peace, peaceable;
change, changeable.

4 In one-syllable words with a short vowel sound you must double the last consonant before adding a suffix beginning with a vowel, e.g.
stop, stopping,
hop, hopped.

5 In words of more than one syllable, if the last syllable has only one vowel, you must double the last consonant before adding a suffix beginning with a vowel, e.g.
admit, admitted;
begin, beginning.

6 If a word ends in consonant plus 'y', you must change the 'y' to 'i' before adding a suffix, e.g. pony, ponies.

7 When a word ends in 'f', you sometimes change the 'f' to 've' before adding 's', e.g. loaf, loaves.

8 If a word ends in a consonant plus 'y', you change the 'y' to 'i' and add 'es' for the plural, e.g. lorry, lorries.

9 The words 'all', 'well', 'full' and 'till' always drop one 'l' when added to another word, e.g. always, welcome, fulfil, until.

10 You use 'or' at the end of a word when you mean 'one who' or 'that which', e.g. actor, inspector. (But, simple verbs ending in 'e' become 'er', e.g. bake, baker.)

Quick Questions

In the following passage some words have been underlined that are incorrectly spelled. Rewrite the words, spelling them correctly.

The <u>ponys</u> were in the <u>feild</u> eating grass. They were <u>hopeing</u> that their riders would be <u>peacable</u>. Someone was <u>stoping</u> at the gate. The boy looked up at the roofs of the stables. They <u>allways</u> looked golden in the sun. The boy waited for his riding <u>instructer</u>.

Now work out which pattern applies to each spelling error.

Spelling patterns also apply to words when they change their grammatical function in a sentence. Using the same stem but changing the ending of a word alters the kind of word it is. Look at the following:

Noun	Adjective	Verb	Adverb
import<u>ance</u>	import<u>ant</u>		import<u>antly</u>
comple<u>tion</u>	complet<u>e</u>	to complet<u>e</u>	complet<u>ely</u>

What you need to know

1   **Prefixes**   These are *opening* sections of words that affect the meaning of a word. *Psycho* is a prefix. What does it mean?
How many different words can you think of that use this prefix?
Ask yourself the same questions about 'physio' and 'auto'.
Try to find other prefixes.
Some prefixes change a word from positive to negative e.g. 'un' and 'dis'.
Write down as many words as you can that use these prefixes.

2   **Suffixes**   These are *closing* sections of words like the ones we looked at earlier. They can change the function and meaning of a word and their spelling needs to be learned.
Here are some more examples:
-ness,
-able,
-ible,
-ibility.

You will gain marks for the use of accurate punctuation in the writing sections of these papers. Revise the essentials.

What you need to know

1   **Capital letters** and **full stops** clarify meaning. Try writing the following out using capital letters and full stops to clarify meaning.
the bike was damaged in the morning we decided we would move it

2   **Commas** help to clarify meaning within a sentence, e.g.
Jane, who is a pilot, listens to the weather forecast.
Use them to separate items in a list, e.g.
Juliet feels upset, confused and very much in love.
Do not use commas if you need full stops, e.g. 'I am hungry, I will eat a sandwich' is wrong because there are two sentences.
It should read *I am hungry. I will eat a sandwich.*

3   **Semi-colons** link two statements together when the subject of each statement is the same or closely linked. So, you could write *I am hungry; I will eat* because you have used two statements that are closely connected.

4   **Colons** are used to tell the reader that a list or quotation is to follow, e.g. *Romeo is introduced as a sad person: 'Ay me, sad hours seem long…'*

5   **Speech marks** are used around the words spoken by a character.

6   **Apostrophes** are used to indicate possession, e.g. *The cat's ball.* They are also used when a letter has been missed out, e.g. *don't.*

Examiner's tips

tip 1   The words inside speech marks always end with a punctuation mark which must come inside the closing speech mark, e.g. 'Go away!' she said.

tip 2   If the sentence carries on after the speech marks, use a small letter even if the speech ended in an exclamation mark, as in the example given above.

tip 3   When writing 'its' only use an apostrophe when you mean 'it is', not for possession.

You might be asked to write a letter. The question might look like this.

Write a letter to your local newspaper, complaining about the lack of activities for young people in your town.

In your letter you could write about:

- the present state of facilities for young people;
- what you think they need;
- why you think it would benefit the whole community if young people were helped;
- what readers of the newspaper could do to help.

Examiner's tips
tip 1   Set your letter out correctly.
tip 2   Make sure you write in a lively style, but be careful not to sound cheeky or jokey.
tip 3   Remember that your audience is the local people who read the newspaper, so imagine you are writing it for your parents to read.
tip 4   Spend some time before you start on the actual letter in writing down in note form the points you want to make.

What you need to know

How to set out a formal letter

(Your address)
2 The Widgery
Stanton Liddle
Wotney
Suffolk
IP15 3RR

10 April 2000

Roger Scrutles
The Editor
The Wotney Globe
3 High Street
Wotney
Suffolk
IP14 1AA

Dear Mr Scrutles

....
....
....
....
....
....
....
....
....

Yours sincerely

Your signature

Your name printed clearly

How to write notes to prepare your letter

Paragraph 1   present facilities appalling because
- youth club closed down
- playground vandalised
- streets dangerous at night

Paragraph 2   they need
- youth club to be open regularly
- money spent on facilities in youth club
- playground redesigned and guarded
- other facilities like cinemas/libraries/churches to be more welcoming

Paragraph 3   It would benefit everyone because
- young people off the streets
- not at risk from drugs, etc.
- older people not in fear of them

Paragraph 4   what readers can do
- ask councillors, MPs, etc. to help
- write in to paper if they agree
- volunteer to help at youth club, etc.

Examiner's tips

How to write your letter in an appropriate style.

tip 1 Set your letter out in the way shown on page 21.

tip 2 Write your letter clearly in paragraphs.

tip 3 Show that you can use full stops and commas correctly.

tip 4 Use colons (:) and semi-colons (;) like this:
There are several actions which could be taken to help the situation: the playgrounds could be cleaned and redesigned; they could be patrolled during the day; they could be locked at night-time.

tip 5 Begin some of your sentences with words such as those used here:
- *Although this may involve the spending of a good deal of money, …*
- *However much we may wish things were different, …*
- *Some people might say, …*
- *On the one hand, … On the other hand, …*
- *It could be argued that …*
- *Given this situation, …*
- *Why is this the case? There may be several reasons. …*
- *These are the reasons why I am suggesting that …*
- *To sum up, I believe that …*

tip 6 Your letter will be marked for the accuracy of your spelling, punctuation and grammar, as well as for the quality of the ideas you put into it. Save some time at the end to check your work.

You might be asked to write a story. The question might look like this.

Write about someone who has the experience of being left out of a group or gang.

In your story, you could write about yourself or someone else, or base your writing on a real or imaginary experience.

How to write your story

Examiner's tips		
tip 1	**Characters**	Invent two or three characters. Do not write about large numbers of people. Make them different from each other. Use **DAD** (**D**ialogue, **A**ction and **D**escription) to create the characters.
tip 2	**Setting**	Describe a place where the story takes place.
tip 3	**Plot**	Plan your beginning, middle and end before you start. Think of a surprising, exciting or unusual ending which will interest your reader.
tip 4	**Spelling Punctuation Grammar**	Remember that you will be marked on accuracy as well as on how well you tell the story. Leave time to check through your work at the end.

Writing a plan for your story

Spend the first few minutes of your time planning out your story – like this.

Characters   John – boy who wants to join gang – nervous – likely to do something stupid to prove that he is fit to join
Gary – gang leader – enjoys John's nervousness – bully – bullied by own dad at home
Justine – scared of Gary – joins in making fun of John – you think she'll side with John in the end, but she doesn't

Setting   derelict building site – gang headquarters

Plot   Gary gets John to jump from one roof to another to prove he's good enough to join the gang
John, after hesitation, does it

Justine makes John think she's going to congratulate him, but doesn't
Gary just about to speak, when he hears dad shouting for him – goes off
Justine goes with Gary
John left alone, as rest of gang follow Gary and Justine

Using DAD to create characters

Let's create the character of John, using **DAD**.

Dialogue   Make John say things that will tell the reader what he is like.
For example: *'I want to join, … y'know, the gang,' he muttered.*
'OK,' he said, looking up at the roof, 'How do I get up there?'
'Right, I did it. Now what?' he asked, with his first grin of the day on his face.

Action   Make John act in a way that tells the reader what he is like.
For example: *He looked down and kicked the gravel at his feet. He took a deep breath, closed his eyes, stretched out his arms … and jumped. He stared up into the sky, alone, blinking away the tears.*

Description   Describe John in a way that tells the reader what he is like.
For example: *A boy walked up, skinny, with a leather jacket too big for him: probably his brother's cast-off, they all thought.*

Examiner's tips

tip 1 Before you go into the exam, think of the kind of characters you might write about in your story. Make sure you can spell some of the words you might want to use about them, e.g.
shy, abrupt, muttered, threatening, withdrawn, excited, aggressive.

tip 2 Think of words that you will be able to use instead of 'said', e.g.
stammered, mumbled, shrieked, replied, sneered, ventured.

tip 3 Make sure that you can punctuate speech, e.g.
'I don't know,' he replied.
'Why,' he wondered, 'do you want to know?'

tip 4 Write in paragraphs. Make a new paragraph whenever a different person starts to speak. In other writing, make a new paragraph frequently.

tip 5 Don't always use 'then' to connect one event to the next. Try other words and methods.
For example:
Instead of
He turned away. Then John said …
write
He turned away. Staring at his back, John shouted…
Instead of
He stretched out his arms. Then he jumped,
write
He stretched out his arms. He jumped…
or
He stretched out his arms. Down below, they all saw him leap into empty space.
Be adventurous in your writing!

You might be asked to write a newspaper article. The question might look like this.

Write an article for a local newspaper about an accident involving a child who wanted to join a gang.

Make what you write sound and look like a newspaper story.

Examiner's tips

tip 1   Look at newspaper articles before you go into the exam. Look at how they are set out and at the language they use.

tip 2   Work out what your story is going to be about.

tip 3   Work out what your headline and subheadings are going to be.

tip 4   Work out who is going to be quoted in your article and how you will refer to them.

Writing a plan for your newspaper article

Who?   John Williams, 15, schoolboy

What?   Fell from roof

Where?   Derelict building

When?   Yesterday afternoon

Why?   Gang dare

Planning headline and subheadings

GANG DARE GOES WRONG

Hospital dash
Eye witness
Troubled parents
Why not at school?
Bright boy
Police vigilant

Using your plan to create the article

Examiner's tips

tip 1   Use your headline and subheadings to create paragraphs in your article.

tip 2   Always begin your article with a one- or two-sentence summary of the whole story. That will be your first paragraph.

tip 3   Remember that, whenever you introduce a person into your article, you must give their full name and say how old they are. You should also indicate their job or profession, as in:
Teacher Jane Harrison...
or...
Richard Pierce, the 18 year old trainee electrician...

tip 4   Use plenty of quotes from these people.
Make sure you use speech marks correctly.

tip 5   Use dramatic language where appropriate, as in
He leapt from the building...
rather than
He jumped
or
The family is devastated
rather than
The family is upset...

The article might look something like this:

GANG DARE GOES WRONG

A fifteen year old boy was rushed to hospital yesterday afternoon after falling from a factory rooftop as part of a gang dare which went disastrously wrong.

Hospital dash

Mr William Hardgrave, Consultant Surgeon at St Xavier's Hospital, confirmed that John Williams, of Welcome Street, Dissford, had been brought in suffering from severe head wounds. 'He is in intensive care,' said Mr Hardgrave, 'and lucky to be alive.'

Eye witness

Justine Johnson, 17, confirmed to our reporter that John had been involved in a dare. 'He wanted to join our gang,' she explained, 'and went up to the roof for a dare, to see if he could jump across from one roof to another. I knew it was stupid. I tried to stop him, but he wouldn't listen.' Last night, Justine was being comforted at home by family and friends.

Troubled parents

John's parents, Arthur Williams, 37, and wife Doris, 35, were shocked at their son's action. 'He's always been a good, quiet boy,' said Arthur. 'We can't understand how he got caught up in a thing like this.'

Why not at school?

John should have been at school at the time of the accident. Jenny Smith, Headteacher at Dissford School, said, 'John has never played truant before.'

Bright boy

John is reported to be in high achieving groups at school. Close friends said they were mystified as to why he wanted to join the gang. 'He always works hard and gets good grades,' said classmate Ryan Stubbs.

Police vigilant

A spokesman for Dissford Police has said that they were aware of gang activity in the area, and were instituting regular patrols of derelict buildings.

Writing a newspaper article

Examiner's tip

Don't spend too long making your article look really pretty. It's the quality of your writing which the examiners are interested in.

You might be asked to write an argument. The question might look like this.

Write about how you think young people should be encouraged to get involved in their local communities.

In your answer you could:
- explain why young people sometimes feel isolated from the community;
- describe your experience of living in the community;
- say what you think the community could do for young people;
- say what you think young people could contribute to the community.

Examiner's tips

tip 1   Follow the plan that the question gives to you. Spend the first few minutes writing down in notes what you plan to say.

tip 2   Write in clear sentences and in paragraphs.

tip 3   Vary the way you start sentences.

tip 4   Back up the points you make with examples and personal experiences.

tip 5   Remember to check spelling, punctuation and grammar as you go along and when you have finished.

How to plan your argument

Why young people feel isolated from the community
- nothing to do
- adults criticise what young people like
- nowhere to go
- not enough money to buy what advertisers tell them to buy
- temptation to do illegal things

Experience of living in the community
- adults suspicious/think the worst
- boredom
- pressure to do well at school
- pressure from friends to do what they do
- an actual experience from own life

What the community could do
- make more places accessible to young people
- remember what it was like to be young

- take more time off from working to be with young people
- trust them more in the home
- give them more opportunity to make decisions at school

What young people could contribute to the community
- idealism/energy/time
- new ideas
- time to listen to old people
- voluntary work of all kinds
- already do contribute to arts/music, etc.

How to write in clear sentences and paragraphs

Examiner's tips

tip 1   Read each sentence after you have written it. If it's not entirely clear to you, change it. For example:
'When someone is ignored you can feel isolated from the community because of loneliness' is not a clear sentence.
How could you make it clear?

tip 2   Vary the way you start sentences. For example:
Although that may be true, …
Another point that can be made here is …
I also think it is true that …
However true that may be, …
On the other hand, …
There are many reasons for believing this. Firstly, … Secondly, …
Thirdly, … Finally, …

tip 3   Whenever you move on to a new point from your plan, start a new paragraph.

tip 4   Use colons (:) and semi-colons (;) like this:
There are several actions that could be taken to help the situation: the youth clubs could be cleaned and redesigned; young people could have a hand in running them; they could be patrolled at night-time.

How to improve your spelling

Learn how to spell words that you may be able to use in the writing of an argument, and practise using them in sentences.

certainly	argue	accept
clearly	arguing	acceptable
consequently	argument	unacceptable
eventually	agree	persuade
finally	agreement	persuasion
fundamentally	disagree	persuasive
generally	disagreement	reject
obviously	propose	rejection
possibly	proposal	succeed
principally	suggest	success
	suggestion	successful

Examiner's tip

This is what you have to do to get a a good result for your answer:
- write in a confident, organised way;
- write in an appropriate style and form to argue a case;
- present the arguments clearly;
- develop ideas through a range of grammatical features and the effective use of vocabulary;
- use paragraphs and correct punctuation to make the sequence of ideas clear
- spell complex words correctly;
- write in a fluent and legible handwriting.

When you write your essay about Shakespeare, remember **SCCALAS**

Scene   You will have to write mostly about a particular scene in a particular play. You will know which scene it is before you enter the exam.

Context   You will have to show that you know about the rest of the play. You will need to know what has happened to the characters before this scene and what will happen to them afterwards. You will need to use that knowledge to explain why the characters are behaving as they are in this scene.

Characters   You will have to write about the characters.

Actions   You will have to write about the characters' actions and explain them.

Language   You will have to write about examples of Shakespeare's language.

Atmosphere   You will have to write about the mood and atmosphere of the scene and how it changes, say, from comedy to drama to violence.

Staging   You will have to write about how actors might tackle the scene on the stage.

Examiner's tips

Before you go into the exam:

tip 1   Read and reread the scene many times.

tip 2   Photocopy the scene and write notes on the photocopy.

tip 3   Underline certain words and write next to them what they tell you about the character and his/her actions. Writing about language in this way will help you do well in the exam.

tip 4   Write notes for yourself under the headings SCCALAS. Memorise them.

tip 5   Go and see the play at the theatre. This will help you to write about the staging of the scene.

tip 6   Watch a video version. Better still, watch more than one version, so that you can compare how different directors tackle the same scene. Get the idea that one scene can be staged in many different ways. When you write about the scene, don't write about a video!

tip 7   Remember that your essay will be marked twice: once for the quality of what you say, and again for your standards of spelling, punctuation and grammar. Practise writing clearly about the scene before you take the exam.

SCCALAS: writing about the Scene

Practise writing a paragraph that sums up clearly the most important points of the scene. You should include:
- a summary of the events, in a couple of sentences;
- why the scene is important in the play;
- the changes that occur in the scene, in the plot and in the characters;
- a few words from the scene that sum up what it is about.

SCCALAS: writing about the Context

Practise writing about the context of the scene, i.e., where it fits into the play as a whole. You should include:
- a brief explanation about how the characters came to be in the situation that we see in this scene;
- a brief explanation about how the actions, decisions and attitudes they take in this scene cause them to act the way they do in the rest of the play.
  For example:
  'The hotheadedness that he displays in this scene comes to a climax later when he kills his father and poisons his mother. Once he has taken the action that we see in this scene, there is no turning back for him. He has no choice but to continue with violence and murder.

SCCALAS: writing about Characters

Practise writing about the characters in the scene. You should:
- write only about the characters named in the question;
- quote briefly from the words the characters say, and then explain how those words reveal their personality;
- write about the changes of mind or attitude that the characters go through in the scene;
- explain those changes.

SCCALAS: writing about Actions

Practise writing about what the characters do. You should include:
- a very brief summary of what they do;
- an explanation, or a few possible explanations, as to why they do it;
- a description of the effect their actions have on others in the scene;
- an explanation of why the actions are important in the play as a whole.

SCCAL<u>A</u>S: writing about <u>L</u>anguage

Practise writing about the language of the scene.

- Choose a few important words or lines before you go into the exam. Make sure you can write about them;
- Don't translate them into modern English: say what the effect of the language is. For example: 'When Romeo says: "I am Fortune's fool!" he shows that he realises he has done something disastrously wrong in killing Tybalt. The words also show, however, that he does not want to take responsibility for his actions. He prefers to blame Fortune for what has happened. I think this makes him seem a rather weak person, ready to cry and complain and to blame anyone rather than himself.'

SCCAL<u>A</u>S: writing about <u>A</u>tmosphere

Practise writing about atmosphere by:

- picking out some important words from the scene, such as 'blood' or 'obey' and writing about how those words set the theme of the scene;
- writing about the changes in atmosphere, which will always be there in any scene from Shakespeare;
- explaining why Shakespeare wants to change the atmosphere in this way.

SCCALA<u>S</u>: writing about the <u>S</u>taging

Remember that this a play, designed to be watched in a theatre rather than studied at a school desk! Practise writing about:

- what you might see at certain moments in the scene, if you were watching a performance in the theatre;
- the actions that an actor might perform when saying a particular line;
- how the theatre director could build up the atmosphere of comedy or violence by having the actors perform particular actions.

Examiner's tips

Remember spelling, punctuation and grammar.

tip 1   Practise writing clearly and accurately before the exam.

tip 2   Organise your writing into paragraphs.

tip 3   Choose the words you use carefully. Have some words already in your head: words to describe characters, actions and language, and know how to spell them. For example: Romeo = hotheaded/selfish/thoughtless.
Actions = climax/disaster/consequences.
Language = highflown/romantic/excessive.

Paper 1

Remember

- At the beginning of this test, you have **15 minutes** to read the paper and make notes but you must not start to write your answers until you are told.

- Then you have **1 hour 30 minutes** to write your answers.

- You should answer **all** the questions in Sections A and B. Then choose **one** question only from Section C.

- You should spend about
  10 minutes on question 1
  20 minutes on question 2
  20 minutes on question 3
  40 minutes on question 4.

- Check your work carefully.

- Ask your teacher if you are not sure what to do.

Section A

Read the following story. Then answer question 1 **and** question 2.

My father tried to help me with my homework. He sat hunched over a textbook and I stood by the arm-chair looking over his shoulder, struggling to follow his reasoning. The hands of the clock rushed round and hardly anything would be done. There were awful pauses, with my father sitting motionless, breathing heavily. I tried to bluff by agreeing with him, to try to hurry him on to an answer, but he kept catching me out.

'It's no good if you don't understand it,' he told me. 'How are you going to learn it like that?'

It was useless telling him that if I did not have most of the problems done or something on paper to show, I should be caned for laziness. He wanted me to understand them, once and for all. He was patient and thorough. I knew I would never understand compound interest and problems with trains travelling at different speeds in opposite directions.

In despair I would stare at my mother. If she was worried, uncertain of what to do, she flew into irritation. 'Help the lad,' she cried at my father. 'Can't you help him?'

'That's what I'm doing!' he shouted back. 'Trying to get him to grasp it!'

'There isn't time for all that. What d'you have to be so long-winded for? Just do them. Oh, I wish I could do sums!'

'How about tomorrow night?'

'He'll be in a mess again, won't he? He'll be back again tomorrow night, you daft –'.

'Rubbish!' my father cried.

I stood with a set face. It was finished now. My father had pushed the textbook off his knee and let the pencil drop. In the morning I should be caned.

I must have been twelve when I stayed away for six days one November because of more trouble with my homework.

My mother gave me the packet of sandwiches as usual and I put them in the satchel against the horrible exercise books. I had finished two problems out of six, and even those were wrong. I did not know what I was going to do.

It was Monday morning. There was a soft drizzle blowing into my face. As I sat on the bicycle I felt the tiny drops of moisture catching in my eyelashes. I was alone. No one could help me.

Ahead of me, at the end of the street where I lived, the colours fluttered down the traffic lights, orange and then green. That was the way I went. Instead, I started to pedal in the opposite direction, towards the country.

I rode along in a queer, empty state. My crime was too ghastly to think about, yet it blotted everything else out. I should never be able to go back now, after this. There was no solution. I was cut off from the school, the teacher, my classmates, my mother and father, everybody.

I looked around and was startled because there was no longer a street, or any buildings. I was going across the common already. It seemed incredible. I had been travelling for over ten minutes without watching where I was going. I kept on, riding slowly. This was not the common near Memorial Road, but another one, where I had often played when I was at my first school. It had only happy associations.

The road let me out across the raw, scrubby ground, open and flat on either side, except for a few hollows choked with gorse and brambles. I was hardly conscious of pedalling. The wheels spun under me steadily, with the familiar clear knocking sound coming out of the bottom bearing, in the silence. The noise comforted me a little, banging away cheerfully, as if this were a normal journey.

Something made me turn the handle-bars suddenly to the right, and I bumped over the low kerb and started jolting along a faint track on the wintry grass. There were bare patches worn by boys playing cricket, and I noticed some charred pieces of wood in a circle of ash, left by a tramp.

Finally I stopped in a hollow. I sat for a long time in a stupor, all blank inside. The slight rain was almost finished. Drops had collected under the gorse bushes, hanging very still on the points.

After a while I got stiff, so I pushed up the little slope to level ground, then went on towards the aerodrome. How strange to be here now, on this grass where I used to play when I was careless, happy! All at once I felt desperately sorry for myself, lonely and cold, and I wanted to cry. The bitter tears came, hot on my face, which I knew looked haggard and old. I thought of the joy of owning a bicycle, the far-away happiness of summer days on the common, and how it had ended in this. It was unbearable. I rode on, blindly staring until my front wheel hit a big jagged stone and I nearly fell off.

I was afraid to go back into streets, where people might notice me with my satchel. When I thought it was dinnertime I ate my sandwiches, sitting in a lane. At last I felt certain it had gone half-past four, and asked a woman going into a cottage. It was only three.

From *Running Away* by Philip Callow

Answer question 1 and question 2. Remember to spend less time on question 1 than the other questions. Refer to words and phrases in the passage to support your ideas

1 **What impressions do you get of the boy's personality?**
   In your answer you should comment on:
   - the way the boy behaves;
   - the way the boy thinks.

6 marks

2 **How does the writer make you share in the boy's thoughts and feelings?**
   In your answer you should comment on:
   - the way the boy is described;
   - the way he reacts to his problems;
   - the way the writer describes the boy's surroundings.

11 marks

Section B

Read this poem carefully, then answer question 3. Refer to words and phrases in the poem to support your ideas.

Interruption to a Journey   by Norman MacCaig

The hare we had run over
Bounced about the road
On the springing curve
Of its spine.

Cornfields breathed in the darkness,
We were going through the darkness and
The breathing cornfields from one important place to another.

We broke the hare's neck
And made that place, for a moment,
The most important place there was,
Where a bowstring was cut
And a bow broken forever
That had shot itself through so many
Darknesses and cornfields.

It was left in that landscape.
It left us in another.

3   **How does the poem show that the interruption to this journey was
    very dramatic?**
    In your writing you should comment on:
    *   what the poem tells you about the changing feelings of the people
        involved;
    *   how the poet uses language to bring the situation to life;
    *   your ideas on why the poet wanted to write this poem.

11 marks

Section C

This section of the paper is a test of writing .You will be assessed on:
- your ideas and the way you organise and express them;
- your ability to write clearly, using paragraphs and accurate grammar, spelling and punctuation.

Choose **ONE** of the following:

4 EITHER

a) Imagine that you are a parent, worried about the pressure put on your child by the amount of homework the school is giving.
Write a letter to the headteacher, saying why you think the amount of homework should be reduced.
Write an address for the headteacher at the top. Begin your letter *Dear headteacher* and end it with *Yours faithfully* and your signature.
In your letter you could write about:
- the effect of the pressure of homework on your child;
- why you think homework should be reduced;
- what you think young people should spend their time doing instead of homework;
- how you would make sure that education standards did not fall.

OR

b) **Write about a child who runs away from home.**
You could:
- write about a real or imaginary event;
- try to build up a feeling of suspense or tension.

OR

c) Imagine that you have been given a chance to talk in a year assembly about the advantages and disadvantages of the motor car.
Write your speech. Come to a decision at the end about whether you think the car is on the whole a good or bad invention.

33 marks

Answers

These answers:

- *are full*
- *analyse the text;*
- *show a clear understanding of the writer's intentions;*
- *give personal opinions which are rooted in the text.*

1   The boy is polite and respectful of his parents. This is made clear in the opening paragraphs of the passage where the boy waits patiently for his father without telling him how desperate he was to finish the sums. The boy was clearly not good at mathematics and he worried a great deal about what the teacher would do. The writer uses the word, 'despair' to highlight how upset the boy was. The boy behaves irrationally when he stays away from school. I think it would have been more sensible to have told his father about his problems. It is fear that makes him irrational. He clearly feels that he has no way out. He knows himself well: 'I knew I would never understand …' and he clearly feels more comfortable alone.

2   In the first paragraph the writer describes the boy as 'struggling', which immediately helps the reader to share the problems of the boy. We can imagine the 'awful' pauses as he waits for his father to finish. We are helped in this by the writer's use of the first person as we see things through the boy's eyes. The boy is described as having a 'set face' which tells us that he knows that the worst has happened and he can do nothing, he is almost fatalistic. The writer shows us how the boy reacts to his problems. He is described as being in a 'queer empty state' as he runs away from school. This tells us that he is blocking out the problem. He cannot deal with it. I feel sorry for him at this point. The writer reminds me of a time that I could not cope by describing the boy's actions in such detail. This feeling is increased by the description of the surroundings. Near the beginning the hands of the clock 'rushed round', which helps the reader to feel the worry as time runs out. The writer uses another interesting verb, 'fluttered' to describe the movement of the traffic lights. This suggests a fluidity to the movement and it reflects the sudden decision that the boy makes to run away. The writer uses the weather to emphasise the misery of the boy, 'There was a soft drizzle blowing into my face.' The grass is described as 'wintry' like his feelings. There are 'bare' patches of ground and the area around him is described as 'raw ' and 'scrubby' like his feelings.

Section B

This answer is a full answer that analyses the text and shows appreciation of the poet's use of language. Textual references are used skilfully to justify views given.

3   The poem shows us that the people in the car were thinking about where they had been and where they were going to be:

'We were going …
from one important place to another'

and this suddenly became completely unimportant when they ran over the hare. The place where they had run over the hare was now 'The most important place there was' because of what they had done. The last line suggests that they now felt alienated from the natural world because their unnatural metal machine had destroyed a creature from nature.

The poet uses language to bring the situation to life. The verb 'bounced' helps the reader to 'see' the hare as it is killed. And the description of its spine as being the 'springing curve' on which the hare bounces really shocks the reader into imagining the horror of its death.

I like the line 'Cornfields breathed in the darkness' because it suggests that the fields are alive and also suffering with the hare. The use of this metaphor is effective as it also helps to show the alienation of the humans who have wrecked the peace and the life of the countryside. When the writer talks of a bowstring he suggests that the hare used to move like an arrow shot from a bow and the alliterative use of the 'b' sound almost sounds like crying. Lastly, I would like to comment on the line, 'That had shot itself through so many ...' because the verb 'shot' is often used to show how humans deal with animals but here it is used to describe the speed at which the hare *was* able to move, the speed that has now been removed for ever.

Section C

This sample answer to 4(b) matches the requirements for Level 7, because it:

- *is well organised;*
- *makes the sequence of events clear;*
- *is written in a style which suits the subject;*
- *is interesting;*
- *uses a range of grammatical features, showing that the writer knows many different ways of constructing sentences;*
- *makes good use of vocabulary;*
- *is well paragraphed;*
- *is correctly punctuated;*
- *is correctly spelled.*

Every day when John Andrews arrived home, he found his son sprawled in front of the television. This sight always annoyed him. When he had had a good day at the office, he managed to keep quiet; when the day had been difficult, he shouted, he drew attention to the unwashed dishes in the kitchen, he asked sarcastically about the homework which he knew had not been done.

Today was different.

As he opened the front door, no sound reached him. He walked into the living room. The television was off. No Jonathan. He walked to the foot of the stairs.

'Jonathan! Where are you? Not doing your homework by any chance?'

No reply. John Andrews walked into the kitchen, leaned down to fetch the whisky bottle out of the bottom cupboard, and poured a large one into a clean glass. A clean glass? He's done the washing up, thought John. Maybe I'm getting through to him at last.

It took another fifteen minutes of listening to the radio, pouring himself another one, changing his clothes and reading his mail for John Andrews to realise that Jonathan was not at home.

The wind whipped through his inadequate but incredibly 'cool' jacket as he sat and watched the old men on the green, playing bowls. Jonathan could not imagine his father ever being old and gentle like these men before him, ever being happy playing bowls. Jonathan thought back to his father that morning. He had been his usual grumpy self, not looking at his son, not seeing his father, not caring about the trouble on his face.

Jonathan had almost told him this morning. Walking quickly downstairs, up early for once, he had decided to tell him about the failed exams. That had been before 'Dad' had started. On and on about the washing up, the washing, the bills, Jonathan's inadequacy as a human being, his tardiness, his lack of work ethic.

No, there was no talking to his father. He could never go home.

The cold was beginning to creep into Jonathan's legs and feet. He would have to keep moving. Slowly he rose from the lichen covered park bench with its generations of graffiti on it. He walked down the frosty, leaf-strewn path towards the swings where his father used to push him when he was little. That had been before his mother had left. Now it was not the same.

Moreover, he could not see how it would ever be OK again. He had failed his exams. How could he ever go home?

Three days later, John Andrews heard the doorbell ring. He swallowed the last drop of whisky, and put the glass down amongst the other mess on the living room table. He looked at himself in the mirror: must give the right impression to a visitor. Should have shaved, but too late now.

'Jonathan!' he said, as he opened the door. 'Where have you been? I've been in touch with everyone – your mother – everyone! Still, you're back now. That's what m...'

'Dad,' said Jonathan. 'I've come to get my things. I've failed my exams. I'm going to stay with Auntie Joan and go to college and try to pass them in the summer. I don't want to live here any more. I can see you at weekends if you like.'

'Thanks. I … er … I'd like that,' said John Andrews, standing aside to let his son pass.

Acknowledgements
Every effort has been made to trace copyright holders and to obtain their permission for the use of copyright material.
The authors and publishers will gladly receive any information enabling them to rectify any error or omission in subsequent editions.

The authors and publishers are grateful to the following for permission to use copyright materials:
Page 5: from *The Great Leapfrog Competition*, William Saroyan, from *Reading Stories*, Meller, O'Neill and Paterson, 1987, Chalkface Press, Australia;
Page 6: from *The Good Corn* (abridged), HE Bates, ibid; Page 9: *Tortoise*, David Speechley; Page 39: *Running Away*, Philip Callo, in *Family and School*,
ed. David Jackson, 1971, Penguin, London; Page 42: *Interruption to a Journey*, Norman MacCaig, in *The Rattle Bag*, ed. Heaney and Hughes, 1982,
Faber, London.

Letts Educational
Aldine Place
London W12 8AW
Tel: 020-8740 2266
Fax: 020-8743 8451
e-mail: mail@lettsed.co.uk
website: http://www.lettsed.co.uk

First published 1999
Reprinted 1999 (twice)
Text, design and illustrations: © BPP (Letts Educational) Ltd 1999

Prepared by *specialist* publishing services, Milton Keynes

British Library Cataloguing in Publication Data
A CIP record for this title is available from the British Library.

Printed in Italy

ISBN 1 85758 912 2

Letts Educational is the trading name of BPP (Letts Educational) Ltd